What Kids Did

STORIES OF KINDNESS AND INVENTION IN THE TIME OF COVID-19

Erin Silver

Second Story Press

Library and Archives Canada Cataloguing in Publication

Title: What kids did : stories of kindness and invention in the time of COVID-19 / Erin Silver.
Names: Silver, Erin, 1980- author.
Identifiers: Canadiana 2020030142X | ISBN 9781772601640 (hardcover)
Subjects: LCSH: COVID-19 (Disease)—Social aspects—Juvenile literature. | LCSH: Epidemics—Social aspects—Juvenile literature. | LCSH: Quarantine—Social aspects—Juvenile literature. | LCSH: Helping behavior in children—Juvenile literature. | LCSH: Kindness—Juvenile literature.
Classification: LCC RA644.C67 S55 2020 | DDC j362.1962/414—dc23

Printed and bound in Canada

Second Story Press gratefully acknowledges the support of the Ontario Arts Council and the Canada Council for the Arts for our publishing program. We acknowledge the financial support of the Government of Canada through the Canada Book Fund.

ONTARIO ARTS COUNCIL
CONSEIL DES ARTS DE L'ONTARIO
an Ontario government agency
un organisme du gouvernement de l'Ontario

Canada Council   Conseil des arts
for the Arts   du Canada

Funded by the   Financé par le
Government   gouvernement
of Canada   du Canada | Canada

Published by
Second Story Press
20 Maud Street, Suite 401
Toronto, ON M5V 2M5
www.secondstorypress.ca

PHOTO CREDITS

Mizan Rupan-Tompkins: courtesy of Ronica Rupan-Tompkins

Chelsea Phaire: courtesy of Candace Phaire

Jorge Martínez: courtesy of Gigi Martínez Gracida

Veronika Kolarska: courtesy of Daniela Kolarska

Stephen Wamukota: courtesy of James Wamukota

Iyori Kashiwabara: courtesy of Shuhei Kashiwabara

Rhythm Dance Studio: courtesy of Rhythm Dance

Ellie Myers and Sophie Fogel: courtesy of Shana Faust

Callaghan McLaughlin: courtesy of Kelsea McLaughlin

Good News Now: courtesy of Kaitlyn and Molly Harrington

Hugo Tomkins: courtesy of Katie Tomkins

Quinn Callander: courtesy of Heather Roney

Jeffrey Wall: courtesy of Jeffrey Wall

Arhan Chhabra: courtesy of Arhan Chhabra

Masaka Kids Africana: courtesy of Masaka Kids Africana

Introduction

Everything changed in early 2020. A virus named Covid-19 was spreading quickly all over the world, from country to country, person to person. Suddenly, people were scared of getting sick. Playgrounds were roped off with "caution" tape. Soccer fields were chained shut. School bells stopped ringing. Businesses shuttered their windows and not a single car was out on the roads. People stayed home—it was the only way to protect themselves and each other from a terrible virus.

During the fear and uncertainty came an outbreak of kindness from children across the globe. When people were scared and worried, these kids didn't let their size or age stop them from helping others. Some made masks to protect hospital workers. Others played music or told jokes so neighbors wouldn't feel alone. Some raised money for hospitals, starving animals, and kids in need. Others broadcast the news from their basements and shared good news only.

Against the constant flow of negative virus news, so many kids offered hope, strength, and inspiration when the world needed it most. **WHAT KIDS DID** features children who made a difference when people felt helpless. These are their stories.

Making Her Mark

When **CHELSEA PHAIRE** turned 10, she didn't want gifts at her birthday party. At least not typical gifts, like toys or even a new bike. The little girl from Connecticut had another idea. She asked guests to donate art supplies instead.

Art had always been a hobby, but when her favorite swim teacher died from gun violence, art became her therapy. It helped her manage her feelings and get through a hard time. With the help of her parents, Chelsea created Chelsea's Charity and collected as many markers, coloring books, and pencil crayons as she could. She and her family packed the art supplies into kits and drove across the United States, personally handing out 1,000 kits to kids in schools, foster care, women's shelters, and homeless shelters. Chelsea even taught them her favorite drawing techniques. She loved meeting new people and showing them how art can help.

Then came coronavirus. Chelsea couldn't hand out kits when kids needed them most. But just because she couldn't meet other kids face-to-face didn't mean she couldn't help. Chelsea geared up again. She spread the word through social media and fundraised, gathering more supplies than ever before. She created over 1,500 art kits and mailed them to shelters and foster homes across the United States. Chelsea also posted video messages, telling students online: "Art is important to me because no matter how bad I'm feeling...my art supplies are always there for me...so no matter what happens, know that art is a start!"

She knows how much her efforts can help during a crisis. "It means a lot because of the coronavirus," Chelsea said. "It's just really nice to know kids are helping kids during this really stressful time. It really makes me feel happy."

One day, Chelsea hopes to hit the road and hand-deliver her art kits again. Her goal is simple: "Now my dream is to meet every kid in the entire world and give them art."

Changing the Way We Touch

The coronavirus pandemic struck San Francisco, California when **MIZAN RUPAN-TOMPKINS** was 12 years old. It was the first city in the United States to go into lockdown and everyone was scared of getting sick.

Day after day, Mizan watched his parents use their sleeves to press buttons. Sanitizer was running low. A thinker and tinkerer, Mizan's brain wondered...how could people touch things more safely?

He set to work, using his 3-D printer to design a pocket-sized device to help people press elevator buttons, use an ATM, and open doors without having to use their fingers. Others had designed hooks or knobs, but Mizan kept thinking.

"There had to be a better way, a better design, and a way to reduce germ exposure for people," he said.

Now, with the whole world in quarantine and people afraid to open doors or touch surfaces, he had a solution. He called his new invention the Safe Touch Pro Handle. The gadget is made with eco-friendly, plant-based material and it's antimicrobial, which means it kills bacteria. Mizan created a website and began selling the product online. Hundreds of people have bought his invention, from health-care workers to people worried about the virus. Each one takes 30 minutes to make, so Mizan is busy.

"I really made it for my parents and now it's helping everyone," he said.

Even after the pandemic, Mizan believes the Safe Touch Pro Handle will be helpful since people will still be careful about what they touch.

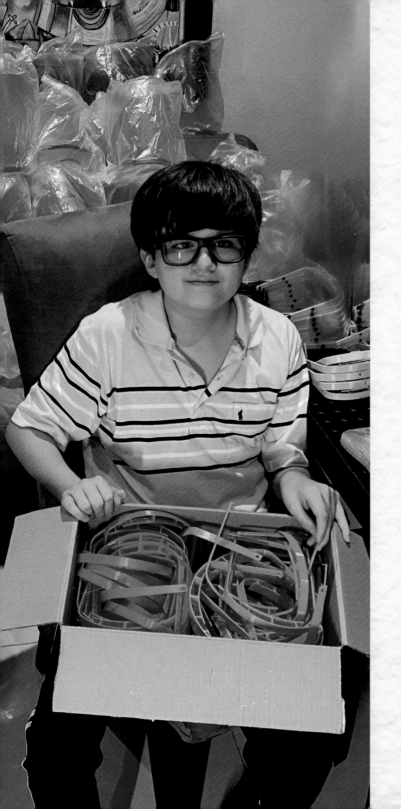

Shielding Health-Care Workers from Covid-19

At 12 years old, **JORGE MARTÍNEZ** wanted what everyone else did for Christmas: a 3-D printer. He taught himself to use the high-tech machine and created small robot figures for his friends. He sold them for 30 pesos ($1.35 USD), 40 pesos ($1.80 USD), or 60 pesos ($2.70 USD), and managed to save 1,000 pesos ($45 USD) in six months.

Then came the coronavirus. Patients poured into hospitals all over the world—including in Oaxaca, Mexico, where Jorge lives with his family. Jorge was very worried when he heard that doctors didn't have enough protective face masks to

shield themselves from sick patients. Born with an eye condition that required him to endure seven years of treatment and four hours of daily eye exercises to avoid losing his sight, Jorge really cared about protecting these doctors.

He leaped into action. Jorge used his entire savings to buy all the materials he'd need to print plastic visors for local health-care workers. "The model I created aims to safeguard doctors facing the dangerous virus," said Jorge. "The face shield I made covers the wearer's eyes, nose, and mouth."

Even his older sister, Gigi, was impressed. "Jorge started the project with his savings with the aim of helping one hundred doctors, since that was all he was able to afford," said Gigi. "He never imagined that this small action would touch the hearts of many people around the world, raising awareness, and inspiring many other children and adults to join in by doing the same."

Not only did Jorge's masks motivate others to make them, he also spurred people to contribute to his cause. Thanks to these donors, Jorge was able to make more than 1,500 masks during the pandemic.

"For me, my little brother is a warrior," Gigi said.

Jorge was just hoping to help. "I'm sad because I saw the news about our doctors and health workers not having enough personal protection equipment to treat patients with Covid-19," said Jorge. "I hope this design helps them save lives and save the world."

The Healing Power of Music and Fitness

VERONIKA KOLARSKA might be from Toronto, Ontario, but she helped people around the world during the pandemic. Veronika, 13, and her friends organized a support group at their middle school to help younger students adjust to life in quarantine. They put on weekly online puppet shows, concerts, and guessing games to entertain kids from Grades 2 to 6.

A musician who plays violin, piano, recorder, guitar, and ukulele, Veronika was involved with a handful of other young musicians through Explorer Hop's Teen Entrepreneurs Program.

She played in the Together Apart Orchestra, sold tickets, and helped with advertising to raise money for Musicians Without Borders.

"We believe that music can heal, and through the power of music, we can help everyone during this challenging time," said Veronika. "Having a musical education gives people the power to get through anything."

Veronika and the Together Apart Orchestra sold out two virtual concerts to worldwide audiences, and were able to provide 1,200 music lessons to children in Rwanda, Africa.

Stuck at home and unable to practice in the pool with her competitive synchronized swim team, Veronika needed a way to stay active during Covid-19. Along with teen entrepreneurs from all over Canada, she organized two online global fitness workouts to get people exercising at home. Veronika even taught fitness classes for the event.

"We raised enough money to provide Doctors Without Borders with the funds to safely deliver seven thousand life-saving vaccines or enough to deliver thirty babies safely," said Veronika. The organization sends doctors to help people in violent, impoverished areas all over the world.

"It's been very challenging for me, and for everyone, to be isolated—to be apart from friends, family, and school," said the teen. "It felt great to give a helping hand to others and save lives."

Washing His Hands of the Pandemic

STEPHEN WAMUKOTA heard the president of Kenya tell people that hand washing could help prevent the coronavirus from spreading. It gave the nine-year-old an idea. Stephen went to the backyard.

"On the first day, I collected timber, nuts, and nails, and on the second day, I started making the machine. I continued on the third day, and on the fourth day, my dad helped me to finish it."

Even though his dad, James, had planned to make a window with the wood, he was "very proud" when he saw what his son had done: Stephen had invented a semi-automatic wooden hand-washing machine.

James helped Stephen make a few adjustments, and then the machine was ready to use.

One foot pedal squeezed out soap and the other tipped a bucket to pour water, so people could wash their hands without having to touch

anything with their hands. It also dispensed hand sanitizer.

"This device can be used in Kenya and all over the world because the disease is everywhere," said Stephen.

When James posted a video of Stephen's invention on Facebook, people took note—including the President of Kenya. He awarded Stephen the Presidential Order of Service. Stephen became the

youngest of 68 people to receive the honor. He was also awarded a primary and secondary school scholarship from the governor of Bungoma County in Kenya, where Stephen lives with his parents and five siblings.

Stephen couldn't be happier. He dreams of being an engineer when he grows up. "I now have two machines and I want to make more."

Virtually Unstoppable

When **IYORI KASHIWABARA** was three years old, he asked his dad for a computer game called Minecraft.

At the time, his father, Shuhei, didn't understand why kids enjoyed it so much, but recently, he learned firsthand.

Sad that school in Japan had been canceled because of Covid-19, and realizing he'd miss out on his Grade 4 graduation ceremony, Iyori, now 10, picked up his gaming controller. With the help of a handful of friends online, they used Minecraft to build a pixilated but elaborate setting for a graduation ceremony. It included a stage, seating, podium, red carpet, and a banner that read "Summer."

After hours of hard work, graduates were invited to the virtual ceremony in the school gym. One by one, Iyori and his classmates walked up to the stage to receive their certificates. There were even graduation speeches. Now, all the kids were officially promoted to the next grade.

Shuhei happened to check in on his son as the ceremony took place.

"What are you doing?" he asked.

"We all decided to have a graduation ceremony together!"

"Oh? Awesome!"

His dad then tweeted a video of Iyori giggling as he watched the virtual ceremony on his computer.

"It's funny, is it not?" asked Iyori.

Shuhei was surprised at how Iyori and his friends used Minecraft "beyond imagination." He was also "impressed that the ceremony was built with

such details from the entrance to the exterior." Perhaps most impressive was how the kids designed the ceremony themselves, without any help from teachers.

After the ceremony, Iyori and his friends played online together for the rest of the day. Meanwhile, the video Iyori's dad tweeted quickly went viral. It even inspired others to create their own virtual graduation ceremonies, since nobody could attend in person.

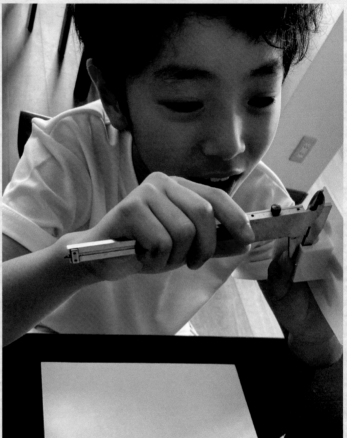

Iyori is "delighted" to have inspired others, but he's busy with other things. "Other than games, he likes crafts, field work, and music," said his dad. While he can't imagine the future right now, Shuhei said, "I expect my son to create an environment where he can interact with the world and do what he likes with his good friends."

Competitive Dance Team Find Their Rhythm

THE JUNIOR GIRLS at Rhythm Dance Studio in Toronto, Ontario love to compete. They have danced together for years, practicing countless hours every week as part of a team. But when their dance studio was closed and competitions were canceled, the girls felt sad. They were even a little scared.

"We saw all the people struggling during these hard times," said 10-year-old dancer Joey Sieradzki. "We thought it would be a great idea to organize a dance-a-thon so we could dance all day with our friends, raise money for hospitals fighting Covid, and bring happiness and joy."

The tight-knit group of 13 girls, ages 10 to 13, divided themselves into committees. Some created the logo while others handled social media, fundraising, and planned a schedule for the online dance-a-thon. They called it Dance for a Chance. It was cute and catchy. When they emailed friends and family and appeared on the news asking for sponsors, people responded.

"Originally our goal was to raise $1,500, and we had that in ten minutes," said Chloe Wise, another dancer.

"So then we had a goal to reach $10,000, and we did it in three days," added Joey.

In the end, Dance for a Chance raised over $20,500 for the University Health Network Emergency Covid-19 Relief Fund. The fund was created to support doctors as they worked to help people with the virus.

"We're really proud of ourselves and that we could make a difference and help so many people," said Joey.

"The girls trained all year to compete," said Joey's mom, Elise. "They missed working together as a team. The dance-a-thon gave them a goal, kept them motivated, and I think even they were surprised at what a bunch of kids could achieve when they work together."

Crafty Kids Deliver Kindness On the East Coast

It was the peak of the pandemic when mysterious presents began popping up on neighbors' front lawns in the small community of Bethel, near Charlottetown, Prince Edward Island. There were handmade wind chimes, bird houses, painted rocks, and wooden signs with inspirational words.

Who was responsible for this creativity and kindness? By the time neighbors poked their heads out their doors, all they could see were taillights. It was a great East Coast caper until the do-gooders were caught red-and-blue handed.

"We plead guilty," said **J.J. TREMBLAY**, 13, when a reporter arrived at his front door. His twin sister, **ELLA**, stood behind him holding a painted blue-and-red lawn mushroom.

For 14 weeks, the crafty kids used all the tools of the trade, from saws and sanders to paint and flour, to put a smile on the faces of their neighbors, many of whom were isolated at home during the lockdown.

The idea took shape—then quickly ballooned—when schools were closed because of Covid-19. J.J. and Ella's grandparents, Jim and Leslie Jordan, devised a daily schedule for the twins. In addition to schoolwork and outdoor play, there was plenty of time for crafting.

"This was just as important as their schooling," said their grandma, Nanny Leslie. "It was something that really showed the twins that the most important thing in life is caring about people. We wanted them to know the true feeling of giving."

In all, the family made 12 different crafts including more than 40 bird houses, at least 20 loaves of cake, and more than 50 personalized rocks. Friday nights were especially busy in

the household since delivery day was Saturday.

Before long, neighbors caught on and waited expectantly to see what craft would be delivered. As thanks, neighbors dropped off craft supplies and gift cards for the twins. J.J. and Ella even received two red maple trees, the tree of the island.

Why did the twins do it? Explained Ella: "Our neighbors are very nice to us and we like to show a bit of niceness to them."

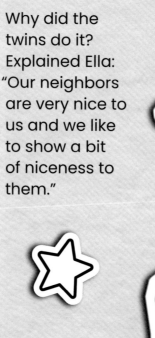

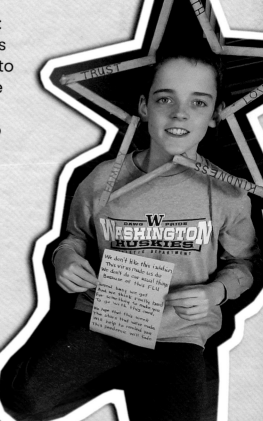

Making Leftovers New Again

ELLIE MYERS and **SOPHIE FOGEL** never have to think about what they're having for dinner. As long as there are leftovers, their families are in luck.

That's because the 12-year-old friends from Brooklyn, New York helped create a cookbook called *Lockdown Leftovers*. It contains about 100 recipes that can be made from leftovers people have in their fridge. The girls donated all their proceeds from the sale of the book to feed hungry animals at the Toronto Zoo. It was a win-win for people and animals.

"I took a young entrepreneur's class and started thinking about what I wanted to make or do for our philanthropy project," explained Ellie. "I thought we could do a leftovers cookbook because lots of people can't go outside to buy food from the grocery store, but they can still make good meals out of stuff we wouldn't normally think of."

Added Sophie: "The book is also helpful to people because you don't have to keep going back to the grocery store during a pandemic and risking your health. It's also good financially because you can just use what you have and not waste money."

The girls insist that any food—even leftovers—can be used in delicious new ways.

"If you have chicken, you can turn it into chicken soup," said Sophie. "If you have leftover fruit or vegetables, you can make it into a smoothie bowl. That way, you're turning what you have into something new and different, and not wasting anything."

Sophie and Ellie worked with a handful of other kids—some as young as nine years old—to create the idea, research recipes, design the book, and publish it online. They chose to help the Toronto Zoo for a great reason.

"Because of the pandemic, nobody was going to the zoo—there weren't any field trips, and nobody could buy tickets on weekends," said Ellie. "We heard there wasn't enough money to buy food for the animals, and we thought it was horrible."

"We really want the animals to have all the nutritious food they need and make sure they're taken care of," said Sophie.

In the meantime, they are each cooking and baking at home, even if they aren't the best at cleaning up afterward!

Making People Laugh, One Joke at a Time

"What do you call a lazy kangaroo? A pouch potato!"

"What's a pirate's favorite letter? Rrrrrr!"

These jokes made it into the comedy lineup at **CALLAGHAN MCLAUGHLIN**'s joke stand. The six-year-old from Saanich, British Columbia wanted to connect with other kids and give neighbors something to laugh about during the pandemic. Instead of their usual lemonade stand, Callaghan and his mom, Kelsea, agreed that a joke stand would be a great way to bring the community together for a laugh while also physically distancing. He set up a table at the end of his driveway and told jokes at a safe distance to anyone passing by.

"There's a lot of stress in the world, and I kind of want to get some smiles on people's faces," said Callaghan.

For a jokester, Callaghan took his job seriously. He opened his stand at 10 a.m. every day, took a lunch break, and reopened the stand in the afternoon. He'd been telling knock-knock jokes and one-liners at home for months, and his family agreed he was ready for a new audience.

People smiled and waved as they passed, but many stopped to tell Callaghan a joke of their own. His classmates and school principal stopped by, as did many elderly neighbors. Even the famous Canadian actor, Ryan Reynolds, heard about Callaghan's joke stand and called him a hero on Twitter. Callaghan loved making people laugh, and he insisted on doing it for free.

"I want people to save their money for other things," he said. "Some people need the money for groceries now instead of jokes."

When asked by a reporter if he had any bad jokes, Callaghan replied, "I don't think I have any bad jokes, but my sister has awful ones!" And if you liked that one, Callaghan says he has 13 or 14 more.

Sisters Share the Good News Only

"Three-two-beep!"

And that's their cue. The *Good News Now* co-hosts were on air.

"With so much focus on the bad news out there," began 15-year-old **KAITLYN HARRINGTON**, "we're here to bring you some of the countless good stories happening in our world, our nation, and our communities."

"So now, here's some good news!" said **MOLLY**, 10, addressing their dad's camera.

Since the pandemic began, these outgoing sisters from Philadelphia,

Pennsylvania have put together a good-news-only newscast from their basement. Their pool table doubled as the news desk, and they even made a GNN logo, theme music, and a Facebook page to post their newscasts. They also shared links to positive stories and wrote back to fans and media outlets, all of whom enjoyed their heartwarming stories at a time when most of the news on TV was frightening.

"It's about all the good news that's happening…. It's a lot of stuff that doesn't get a lot of attention because of the negative news," Kaitlyn explained.

"We wanted to lift peoples' spirits," said Molly.

Both active in theater, playing the role of newscasters was a natural fit. They approached each broadcast with bright eyes and warm smiles. Sometimes, they even wore their favorite Harry Potter T-shirts! It's been a winning formula.

"We thought it was going to be a one-time thing, but everybody seemed to really like it, gave us a lot of feedback, and told us to keep going," Kaitlyn said.

"We ended up getting tens of thousands of viewers, and it's been really amazing," said Molly. "It's fun to just laugh at ourselves when we mess up."

Their effort to focus on good news was so inspiring that they were called community heroes. The girls aren't sure they fit in with Wonder Woman, however.

"I don't think we're heroes," said Kaitlyn. "We're just trying to spread the good news about the heroes."

Boredom-Busting Newsletter Brings Community Together

THE ISOLATION TIMES
The COVID-19 boredom-busting newsletter *by Hugo at number 51*

NEIGHBOUR OF THE WEEK
The neighbour of the week is the world's favourite (well almost)...
Nathan and Talia at No.48! Nathan is turning 9 in 2 weeks and Talia is 6. They go to Greenslopes state school. They also have a baby sister. Her name is Cadence and she is 8 months old.

PUZZLE OF THE WEEK

OTHER WORLD RECORDS
Check out another one of these crazy and strange Guinness World Records.

LOTS OF T-SHIRTS
Talk about a layered look. Ted Hastings from Ontario in Canada, holds the record for the most t-shirts worn at once – an incredible 260, weighing about 75 kg in total! The stunt took a bit longer than usual, dressed in the morning –

JOKES
Joke 1 submitted by Michael at No. 49. Joke 2 submitted by Darren at No. 45.
I threw a boomerang a few years ago. I now live in constant fear.

Why did the chicken cross the road?
We don't know, but hopefully it's one of the 16 reasons to be out of lockdown.

Why do we tell actors to, "break a leg?"
Because all plays have a cast.

BOREDOM TIPS
Here are some fun and easy-to-do boredom tips to keep you entertained!

• If you have a pet, re-create a famous work of art with your pets face instead of the real one! E.g. the Mona Lisa, Painted version.

• Make a workout for every person in the family. (P.S. if you have an annoying family member, make theirs really hard.)

• Experiment with your hair. Mohawks are the best!

We hope you have enjoyed the 4th edition of The Isolation Times!
Next week's edition will include...
• Featured products
• Fun facts, jokes and more boredom tips

THANKS TO EVERYONE WHO HAS SUBMITTED IDEAS THIS WEEK AND THE MYSTERY NEIGHBOUR WHO CROCHETED PUPPIES FOR US. IF YOU WANT TO BE THE FEATURED NEIGHBOUR OF THE WEEK, MAKE SURE YOU JOT DOWN SOME FACTS ABOUT YOURSELF AND JOHN SUBMIT...

PUZZLE OF THE WEEK

5				8	6			1
	2	7	1		6	2		
	7	1					6	
9	1				2	5		

ISOLATION BOREDOM TIPS

Bored in isolation? Why not try some of these ideas to keep you entertained.

• Try baking- Hugo made marshmallow and choc chip cookies! Why don't you give it a go?

• Teach your granny how to floss over time. Trust me, she'll need it.

HUGO TOMKINS was bored at home when his school closed. Just nine years old, he missed playing with his friends and going to school in person.

He was feeling lonely...until he had an idea. "One of my mom's friends was getting a street newspaper in their area and we thought it would be a good idea to start one for something fun to do while we were stuck inside," said Hugo.

He created a newsletter on his computer called *The Isolation Times: The COVID-19 boredom-busting newsletter.* "There were sections with jokes, fun facts, a recipe, and a neighbor or pet of the week," said Hugo, who lives in Brisbane, Australia with his parents and younger brother Lyndon, 6.

Neighbors were invited to come by with information about themselves and put it in the Tomkins' mailbox. One person even donated paper so Hugo could print copies and deliver them to neighbors each week during the pandemic. "We had lots of contributions from everyone!"

People loved receiving their newsletter when it was hot off the press. "We forgot to deliver to a house one week and we got a note from them asking if we were still doing it," Hugo remembered.

He met lots of people during his newsletter run, including neighbors he didn't know before. While Hugo was not looking forward to getting homework again, he is back at school and happy to see his friends. He learned a lot from his experience during coronavirus. "It's important to stay close to your neighbors in a pandemic in case anyone needs anything and it's good to be friends with people who you don't know."

Asked when his byline might appear in *The Isolation Times* again, Hugo's response was direct. "I will start doing *The Isolation Times* again in the next global pandemic, which is hopefully NEVER!"

Even more kids around the world found unique, creative, and amazing ways to help.

THE NDLOVU YOUTH CHOIR from South Africa became famous after performing on *America's Got Talent*. Their music went viral again when the group used songs to teach kids how to safely wash their hands without running water during the pandemic. They also posted helpful videos online to teach people about the virus.

After learning that the elastic bands on face masks hurt health-care workers' ears, 12-year-old **QUINN CALLANDER** from Canada used his 3-D printer to create a special ear guard. His invention was so successful he's since shipped hundreds of ear guards to medical workers all over the world.

When schools were shut, 13-year-old **HIME TAKIMOTO** from Japan used her own money—about 80,000 yen, or $750 USD—to buy the materials she'd need to sew masks for hundreds of orphans and elderly people. She spent about five hours a day making them, and she packaged them individually with the message, "Wash your hands and gargle diligently."

JEFFREY WALL might be a teenager but he's the founder of Golden Age Karate, in Ohio. A young karate master, he teaches karate to seniors at a local nursing home. When the pandemic struck, Jeffrey refused to close up shop. He started a YouTube channel so seniors could continue to learn and stay physically active during quarantine.

JYOTI KUMARI, a teen from India, was stuck far from home with her wounded father when the lockdown was announced. She cycled him 1,200 kilometers (about 745 miles) to his native village. The journey took seven days and was called a "feat of endurance and love" online. After, Jyoti was invited to a trial with the Cycling Federation of India.

ARHAN CHHABRA wanted to help students in India learn during the pandemic. The 15-year-old from Hong Kong set up Project CoVidya to provide education and support to those who needed it. Within a few days, over 500 volunteers had signed up to help tutor online. CoVidya is a combination of Covid-19 and *Vidya*, which means "knowledge" in Sanskrit.

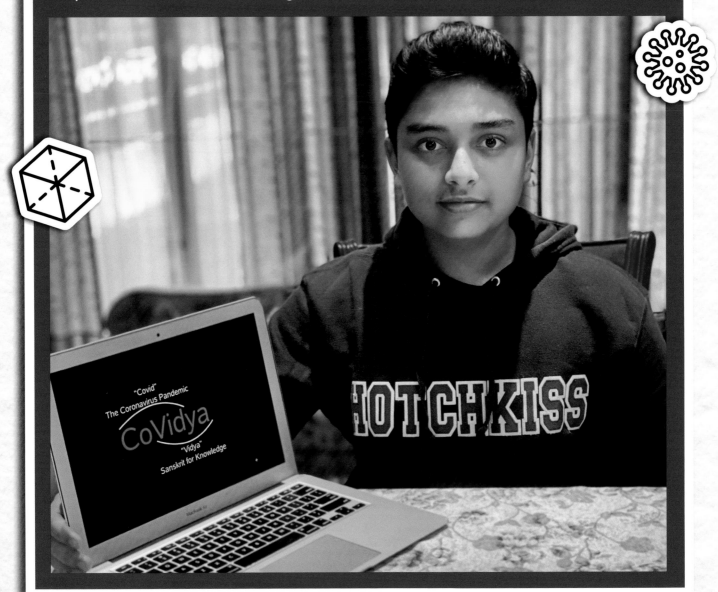

Even though their hockey season was cut short, a young hockey team in Toronto found a new way to work together during the pandemic. **THE FOREST HILL FORCE**, a group of eight- and nine-year-olds, teamed up to raise funds for the Daily Bread Food Bank.

Three Girl Scouts from Virginia Beach had 600 boxes of cookies left when in-person sales were stopped because of Covid-19. The Scouts—sisters **SYLVIE**, 14, **JULIA**, 9, and **PIPER**, 6—launched an online Girl Scout cookie booth. Proceeds from the cookies sold were donated to medical first responders.

Nothing can stop **PIPER SHUMAR** from collecting cans—not even a pandemic. The nine-year-old from Michigan, who once battled a chronic illness, continued to work toward her goal of collecting and recycling enough cans to donate 200 bikes to Bikes for Tikes. The organization gives bikes to kids in need.

A group of talented young orphans in Uganda, called **MASAKA KIDS AFRICANA**, provided hope and information during the coronavirus pandemic. They posted lively and energetic song-and-dance videos encouraging people to wash their hands, avoid touching their face, and "stay home and dance" to protect each other from the virus.

He had lots of schoolwork, but it didn't stop **BEN THORNBURY**, 14, from setting up an advice and support website during Covid-19. The site matched volunteers with people in their rural town in Wiltshire, England who needed help getting food and medicine during the pandemic. The site was inundated with people who wanted to help.